LOVE IS A TANKA

Poems by
Jeanne Lupton

BLUE LIGHT PRESS ❖ 1ST WORLD PUBLISHING

1ST WORLD
PUBLISHING

SAN FRANCISCO ❖ FAIRFIELD ❖ DELHI

Love Is a Tanka

Copyright ©2021 Jeanne Lupton

BLUE LIGHT PRESS
www.bluelightpress.com
bluelightpress@aol.com

1ST WORLD PUBLISHING
PO Box 2211
Fairfield, IA 52556
www.1stworldpublishing.com

BOOK & COVER DESIGN
Melanie Gendron
melaniegendron999@gmail.com

COVER ART
"Night Flowers"
Artist: Paula Lawrie, Instagram

INTERIOR ILLUSTRATIONS
Melanie Gendron

AUTHOR PHOTO
Cathy Cade
Cathy@cathycade.com

FIRST EDITION

Library of Congress Control Number: 2021939056

ISBN: 9781421836980

For Lynne, Dave, Bobby,
Jack, Laurie, Henry,
Anna, Charlotte, Natalie,
AJ, Oliver, Max, Andy, Beth,
and New Baby Tucker

Table of Contents

from *but then you danced* – 2006

weary one, draw near
rest here, and warm yourself
by firelight
put down your struggle awhile
tomorrow, the barricades

• • •

love I've yet to meet
camellias bloom in winter here
and so do I
come soon
the garden is lush in moonlight

• • •

on BART
a woman standing near
has tortilla breath
I want to kiss her
hungry in California

she brings me mangos
from Asia   from the Islands
from the market
many summers have come and gone
always I loved mangos

• • •

two whole hours late
just to bake banana bread
when we could have been
together
but then you danced   you danced

• • •

no footfalls
tell your coming
only
soft clicking
of the bead curtain

your touch
unshrouds the radiance
at my center
I catch my breath
reborn

• • •

after your touch
my body finally fits
full of sky
and mountain meadows
I sleep all afternoon

• • •

not the same
when you came back to bed
at dawn
as when I first awoke
enfolded in your warmth

we imprint dawn
with the image
of our bodies together
the whole day
shaped by love

• • •

that single tear
streaking your beautiful face
because of me
even now
is a downpour in my heart

• • •

dark morning
my harsh words echoing
echoing —
small voices of the rain
tell her the truth of my love

this is the hour
our music discovered
I am mute
without your patient hands
come home and practice

. . .

exquisite dusk
these are the hush, the dimming,
the lull of heartbreak
how this and all my days
will end, in yearning

. . .

61st Christmas
an Irish tenor's love song
makes me cry
not that I was never loved
but I did not care for love

autumn dusk
not even a favorite
old sweater
takes the chill off
my life alone

. . .

in the night
not sleep but hopelessness
claims me
the cat plops himself down
against my back

. . .

in a dream
making love with an old flame
becoming mother
to a swarm of fireflies
he bugs me still

autumn gusts
bring sweet music
from the wind chime
on the porch
of my unfriendly neighbor

. . .

new house
I introduce myself
to neighbors
they introduce
only their dog

. . .

let her go
that lithe summer girl
it's autumn
and she never thought
to linger

60th September
honeybees wild
in yellow blossoms
I was born
for middle age

• • •

how green the green
in the grey light after the storm
how lake the lake
and thistle, thistle
in these hills how me I am

• • •

following
the lakeside trail
into quiet
this step, and this
all there is

from summer hills
we watch
the shooting stars
my last aunt
and I

. . .

a day and a night
in billion-year-old mountains
my door wide
to hear
the white butterflies

. . .

evergreens attend
the old grey stone façade
of the burned church
on this Sunday
snow in the churchyard

snows of yesterday
fall on Appalachian hills
in silence
I watch from tall windows
at eighteen   at sixty

• • •

winter woods are still
but for the crunch underfoot
and that moaning
that creaking high in the trees
stop — hear how they love their life

• • •

I'm the same
as sunshine through the pine
as the pine
as the breeze
in her branches

eucalyptus
in the wind
all
the time
in the world

• • •

crossing the Bay Bridge
with a friend who fears heights
I do not mention
that once, in despair, I
stopped my car just here and jumped

• • •

in a still wood
scattering Father's ashes
at Easter
rising up out of the brush
a wild turkey flies away

in this old photo
see me standing in the shadow
of my father
ash, he casts no shadow now
and I struggle for light

. . .

love yourself
let others catch the overflow
to put them first
will make you thirst, run you dry
it was a lie — love yourself

. . .

woman's wail
from the institution
not me this time
this time out walking free
I bear witness

dark
behind eyelids
nothing
but night sky
of mind

• • •

once
a goddess smiled in the sky
brighter than the sun
through all the dark that followed
and preceded, I had light

• • •

darkness too
darkness is a goddess
close your eyes
she is always with you
there is nowhere that is not your home

from *Just Passing Through* – 2010

when she called
the moon salmon
I saw it
arc upstream
in a river of sky

. . .

wordlessly
my curved spine
tells it all
all the more need
for poems about pain

. . .

breeze
blowing my armpit hair
sparse since chemo
not just to be alive
but to feel alive

meditation
teacher
screams
BE
QUIET

• • •

at senior housing
roars of the Cal football crowd
from across Berkeley
a day so beautiful
solitude turns lonely

• • •

at senior housing
a lover from '67
is my neighbor
in a wheelchair from a stroke
he has a crooked smile for me

my elderly aunt
visits me at senior housing
she sits straight-backed
her most dreaded fate
would be to live in this place

• • •

with cable TV
and rubber draperies
to make it dark
my home's like a motel room
just passing through

• • •

from my balcony
at senior housing
a crone's eye view
of earth and sky
this world I love

Friday night
I watch TV in the lobby
a neighbor
brings me a special treat
his last chocolate Ensure

• • •

the gypsy told me
I belong to the world
I send it poems
and keep to these hills
scribbling in the fog

• • •

when I die
play Bobby Darin's
"Beyond the Sea"
for my soul, always sixteen
looking forward to love

60th September
honeybees wild
in yellow blossoms
I was born
for middle age

from *In the Popular Lane* — 2011

.

in a blizzard
trudging up the pike
for a gallon
of syrupy red wine
wanting poems in a bottle

• • •

faded sign
on a roadside shop
in the country
Antique Chairs
Made Daily

• • •

stuck in traffic
cars zoom past on either side
I realize
I'm in the popular lane
and feel a little better

at evening
honeysuckle breezes
strong iced tea
with my dinner companion
comparing state hospitals

• • •

I wanted a kiss
from that handsome Baptist
on our date
long ago in Tennessee
instead he said, *Pray with me*

• • •

a twinge
of sadness
when
AOL says
Good-bye

I didn't quite hear
the last thing he said
before I hung up
but it might have been
I think it was *I love you*

. . .

for warmth
at the bluegrass festival
I wear his extra shirts
he says I look like a hillbilly
walks a little ahead of me

. . .

there was a day
we walked on the beach
lay down
in a hole in the sand
and slept, lulled by surfsong

Sunday night
I let go of him
give him
back to the city
with more or less grace

• • •

my sick cat
sleeps on the balcony
under the stars
healing while he dreams
this warm autumn night

• • •

sick and alone
in my sixty-sixth autumn
I recall
my mother's cool hand
on my forehead

memoir writers
meet at the senior center
one of us
has Alzheimer's
every week the same story

. . .

a rainy noon
I run across the square
to the cafe
to eat tomato bisque
feeling like a poet

Numbered Breaths – 2011

In memory of
Evelyn Davidson Lupton
1921-1996

one October night
Mother tells me on the phone
she has a year to live
my mother, dying?
I say, *see you tomorrow*

• • •

her house quiet
but for the ticking clock
Mother's tears
she almost never cries
her quiet breaking open

• • •

she has morphine now
says she forgives me
You forgive *me*, I think
but old resentments
begin to ease

taking down
Christmas decorations
Mother has changed
she hugs me
says she loves me

• • •

cancer
support group
too sad for her
all the others
will survive

• • •

forgetting
she bounds out of bed
gasping
strong at seventy-four
except for lung cancer

her hair grows back
fine and soft
after chemo
cancer grows back too
so much to do, and nothing

. . .

the oaks
are green again
in silence
we have tea
and chicken soup

. . .

warmth of sand
Mother gazes at the ocean
for the last time
glory of her body
glory of this world

she feels ill
all I can do
is get my hands
in the cool earth
replant the irises

• • •

leaning on me
in the summer dusk
she picks up twigs
from the yard
says *this dying takes too long*

• • •

midsummer breezes
she breathes through a tube
cancels
the daily newspaper
shows me where her will is

I find her breathless
her face full of panic
her oxygen tube
on the night stand
lost in plain sight

• • •

clover in the lawn
leaves of the old dogwood
two to four months
she says *don't sue the doctor
who said it was arthritis*

• • •

with many friends
champagne and cake
in her hospice room
in tiara and mauve silk
Mother turns seventy-five

my mother
tucked in for the night
the eyes of a child
when I say
see you tomorrow

• • •

between worlds
Mother hunches her shoulders
lifts her arms
sits up again and again
preparing to fly

• • •

Saturday
in the small hours
angels lay her away
bird of paradise
in her garden

funeral director
hands me Mother's urn
brushes off his sleeves
crickets droning
on and on

• • •

in a dream
Mother calls as always
It's me! she says
so happy she can still
reach me by phone

from *Hold High Your Pinkies*
Cha Cha Cha – 2012

winter night
after the reading
the poet
points out for me
all the visible planets

. . .

I pull over
to write down a poem
look up
to see a man on a roof
doing tai chi in the fog

. . .

many people
on the street today
noticed
my lovely purple sandals
or else the trailing TP

in the dining room
women in tight little cliques
stir in me
the old hunger to belong
here at the old folks home

. . .

reading death poems
a sudden desire
to hold
in these hands
my own ashes

. . .

in a dream
I who am childless   and old
birth a baby girl
on waking
fragrance of baby powder

how tenderly
he made love to me
that time
I was pregnant with his child
as never before or again

• • •

we take lessons
in the cha cha cha
he gets mad
because I won't
hold high my pinkies

• • •

Sunday afternoon
I'm with my married lover
at a country inn
a strange woman frowning
asks me how his children are

lonesome in the night
I call to my cat
he gets ready for bed —
takes a pee, gets a drink —
jumps up on the bed

from *Life with Larry* - 2016

my father told me
I would live through a man
I finally found him
my 84-year-old client
who has dementia

• • •

How many shrimp
in this shrimp fried rice?
I saw one.
It's probably
the same one I saw.

• • •

Are my sisters around?
No, they passed away, Larry.
Oh, hell!
I'm sorry to have to tell you.
Are my sisters around?

Where am I?
What am I doing here?
How did I get here?
How long have I been here?
Do I belong here?

• • •

I dose him
with anti-anxiety meds
so that I
don't run screaming
from the building

• • •

cold night
Larry rests on the couch
listening to bluegrass
I cook rice and veggies
to feed him is to love him

silhouetted
against the autumn sun
Larry with dementia
in the pose of The Thinker
his green shirt, his bright heart

• • •

"Meow"
Do we have food for Melba?
I just fed her
"Meow"
Shouldn't we feed Melba?

• • •

He says of me
to the head assistant
when she asks
that he would prefer
someone intelligent

I forget his cane
when we go out to eat
afterwards
as we leave the cafe
he takes my hand in his

from *Radical* – 2016

Thanksgiving dinner
with the relatives
I'm eleventh
at a table for ten
the one without a spouse

• • •

first Thanksgiving
without the relatives
instead
I see a movie
"The Addams Family"

• • •

blue butterflies
someone speaks of them
at dawn
and someone else at twilight
shall I fear or love them?

at seventy
kissing lessons
from a younger lover
she tells me
I'm not improving

• • •

knowing him
is like visiting a stream
in a deep canyon —
the stream and the canyon delight
but the horseflies are biting

• • •

for our honeymoon
we go to his aunt's funeral
in Albuquerque
I take all the photos
of my new husband's family

with her
losing myself again?
walking at lunchtime
in the financial district
wearing a dashiki

• • •

shocked
when the doctor suggests
hearing aids
now I hear myself say
"What?" "What?"

• • •

seismic retrofit
at senior housing
noise and dust
for the rest
of some people's lives

always
wanted to be
a radical
now I am
fat and happy

• • •

enough experience
for a lifetime of poems
but the mists
have hidden the mountains
and valleys of memory

• • •

in this drought
I recall how it rained
most weekends
that spring
when we were lovers

"Institution"

square dancing
the best part of the day
at *State*
sometimes volleyball, yoga
for an hour I'm not crazy

• • •

I visit Dad
in the nursing home
play kickball to win
sitting in a circle
with the old men

• • •

music time
on the dementia ward
I forget
I'm the caregiver
bang the drum, sing loudly

Not previously collected – 2013-2019

rainy Saturday
Muddy on the radio
a sweet ache
that could drive me back
into the arms of Gallo Port

• • •

on the beach
a kind boy says *I love you*
in the moonlight
as I cry
about my bad prom date

• • •

my mother sobbing
good-bye for maybe the last time
as they wave
from their little Kansas porch
Gramps in tears, Gram's jaw set

womb of my own
out of you I birth myself
again and again
morning of my body
old void from which I come

• • •

chemo night
strange noises
from the house
from myself
hot cup of rose tea

• • •

I deposit my week's pay
to my checking account
the teller says
here's your receipt
and this is your little balance

the shampoo girl
offers words of comfort
seeing my red nose
the beautician
smells my eau de Gallo Port

. . .

brandy after work
as we leave the bistro
my proper coworker
and her meek husband
invite me for a threesome

. . .

delivering food
donated by Safeway
to the women's shelter
I'm the volunteer
in the new beaver coat

Great Grandpa Hugh
keeps the Quaker peace
with North,
South, and First Nations
as Winchester changes hands

• • •

Metatanka

my caregiver job
so stressful today
my back hurts
all I want to do now
is write tanka and sip tea

• • •

I read
Yosano, Tawara, Nakajo
Tanka Muse!
Let me go further, risk more
honor my poet ancestors

shall I
take the pen name *hato*
meaning *dove*
but also the noble
pigeon?

• • •

after
a satisfying evening
of writing
I read others' online tanka
confidently editing

• • •

she hands me
that overripe persimmon
so pleased with it
to me it is way past
edible

in the mirror
lit by a dim blue bulb
I see
from long ago
a Mongolian shaman

. . .

mist on the hills
wind stirs the treetop branches
the cheraga says
become one with the view
then thank it

. . .

at a big event
an acquaintance
tells me
how great I looked
the other day

nothing reaches her
until the blues show comes on
then, head bowed, eyes closed
she sways in time to the music
the woman with Alzheimer's

. . .

a woman
praises my tanka
she becomes
quite attractive
to this foolish poet

. . .

I like
the handsome artist
who chats me up
but I show him my tanka
and he says *so what?*

menopause
I stop looking for the man
my father told me
I would live
vicariously through

. . .

Callas on TV
sings Imogene's mad scene
from *Il Pirata*
while the friend sitting with me
sings her own dementia song

. . .

in the dentist's chair
awaiting oral surgery
I hear a song
playing on the radio
The first cut is the deepest

from *These Songs* – 2020

a sense of freedom
lifts me up this morning
out of bed
out of past difficulties
into the new day, new me

• • •

I love my muse
deeper than sex
she invites
my soul's delight
to sing these songs

• • •

on a night
when I can't sleep
raspberries
chamomile tea
and this tanka

in the midst
of writing tanka
in a café
I already want
this happiness again

• • •

Facebook
posts our new relationship
my picture
next to your profile picture
of a caterpillar

• • •

last night
at my retirement reading
so much love
tonight a full moon
and disconsolate yearning

herpes
demon guarding my gate
defends
the treasure within
from the fainthearted

. . .

a sing-along
at senior housing
I envy
The Girl
from Ipanema

. . .

I still think
a man will rescue me —
at 72
when I'm happy enough
at senior housing

in advanced age
attentions from a man
I cannot love
wishing for the boy
I turned down in high school

• • •

regret
eats me like a rat
loneliness
eats me like a lion
I should have said yes

• • •

old man, your true love
was not that girl you longed for
but I
who took you home anyway
for years of Saturday nights

crickets
in the September night
full moon in Pisces
after a day at the coast
I lie in moonlit longing

• • •

between
awake and asleep
sounds spill in
I am a part
of it all

Love is a Tanka – 2020-2021

I find
tuna on the carpet
What's this? I say
she answers with a *meow*
that means *I don't know*

• • •

at 9 a.m.
the sky is dark and red
a neighbor confirms
it's ash from the fires
not the Apocalypse

• • •

flatlands in shadow
as fog rolls in
my cat is gone
from her place
by my pillow

today
I do not need any food
75th birthday
for my next quarter century
I'll be a lovetarian

. . .

first night
without my cat
I stay up late
to avoid the dark
of her absence

. . .

first morning
without my cat
but her little face
is looking at me
from within my heart

to be a woman —
we are made, not born
75 years on
I'm making some progress
toward an open heart

• • •

my sister and I
have known each other longer
than any living soul
I rejoice to travel this road
with my wise companion

• • •

standing
in front of the mirror
asking
am I still a hot babe?
I see Granny looking back

Yo Yo plays Bach
I sit in front of the fire
watch the sunset
through the pines
the old cat on my lap

. . .

nessun dorma
my heart opens at high C
George Floyd is there
the sob of a wild turkey
the cry of a mourning dove

. . .

gazing at the plum tree
i feel Grandmother's love
and my love for her
there in the dappled leaves
in the laden branches

spring evening
early to bed with the cat
to rest
and watch the shadows grow
and the hills light up

• • •

for my cat
who likes order
I make the bed —
at the SPCA
she knew I was her person

• • •

"We're Still Here"
after
so many wasted years
to come to this
peaceful in my little room
with a view of sky and hills

on reading my book
a lifelong friend
tells me
she knew me as a poet
in elementary school

. . .

outside senior housing
my old friend greets me
with *Halleluiah!*
We're still here, she cries
from six feet away

. . .

on the patio
at senior housing
sun and breeze
birdsong and creek murmur
What virus?

I lay bare-breasted
against a bare-chested man
once
after my diagnosis
before the lumpectomy

• • •

chocolate mint
at the local tea room
I warm my hands
on the porcelain cup
a sense of travel

• • •

at the cancer center
the First Nations activist
lying on my table
for a foot massage
weeps, says it's humbling

everything
is more so at night
especially
the bark of a wild turkey
the romance of writing

• • •

Grandma's front parlor
knick-knacks and hand-made doilies
and Great-Grandpa
in his chair, his lipless smile
his teary shining eyes

• • •

a friend's scribbled
Valentine's Day card
the same palsied hand
in Great Grandfather's
birthday cards to me

"bluebird"

my weary friend
one night at Eli's Blues Club
gets up to dance
and, arms floating, hips swaying
becomes who she really is

• • •

her mother smothered her
my mother was distant
our friendship a dance
around *leave me alone*
and *come closer*

• • •

our friendship
isn't helped by the pandemic
no café breakfasts
together like we once had
phone calls fewer and fewer

when the weather's nice
I'll invite her for a walk
in her neighborhood
she'll use her walker
I'll bring my trekking poles

• • •

this friend I love
trusts me with her sadness
her aches and pains
I know other friends call her
The Bluebird of Happiness

• • •

morning
meditation
my thoughts
a small noise
in the vast Silence

at my reading
I try to impress her
with tanka
but she's on the café floor
playing with the service dog

• • •

slow passage

having a nice view
isn't like being out in it
putting one foot
in front of the other
slow passage through this world

• • •

early morning
gloom and chill of early spring
Japanese maples
rhododendron, tulip, iris
poppies, daffodils, orchids

my morning walk
is a laugh in the face
of cancer
schizoaffective disorder
whatever would keep me down

• • •

a warm day
I emerge from cocooning
to walk
around the neighborhood
first perspiration of spring

• • •

tiny yellow balls
on the nearby plum tree
baby plums
no matter what
how I love this world

I wanted power
that only a man could give
so I believed
now I have my own hallelujah
I'm woman

•••

what home means
during a pandemic
just this: boiling eggs
cozy in the kitchen light
warmth on an autumn day

•••

I have outlived
my outlaw black sheep status
I find
I have two sisters again
I have a brother again

Marc

tonight
learning a friend
has died
I read his poetry
to feel him near

. . .

he was calling
every morning
on waking
to share new poems
then he had a stroke

. . .

every call
ended with *I love you*
and *I love you too*
in his poems he leaves us
so much of himself

1958
delighted
that day in 8th grade
to discover
Spanish could express feelings
I could make it my own

• • •

dear Miss Ojeda
in 8th grade Spanish class
You no laugh at me
I no laugh at you
I yearned for Spain

• • •

in the textbook
photo of a woman
in a park in Madrid
typing letters for customers
I wanted to do that

a crow
pecks at the prayer flag
on the balcony railing
flies off with bits of it
for her Buddha nest

• • •

Thursday afternoon
waiting for my clothes to dry
in the laundry room
at Strawberry Creek Lodge
happy for no reason

• • •

sleep eludes me
manic about tanka
I forget
to keep my eyes closed
new work on the way

my ideal life
in a parallel universe
does it really matter
that I haven't done all that?
life as it is — close enough

• • •

my sister paints
a watercolor for me
a winter scene
I see through her eyes
the lovely in the cold

Acknowledgements

I thank the editors of the following journals and books for including my tanka in their pages.

American Tanka, Bottle Rockets, Cattails, Chiron Review, ContemporaryHaibunonLine.com, Eucalypt, Fire Pearls 2, GUSTS, *How to Begin*, Hummingbird, Lilliput Review, Lynx, Modern English Tanka, Moonbathing, Moonset, *Oakland Out Loud, Pandemic Puzzle Poems*, Paper Wasp, Poetalk, raw nervz, red lights, Ribbons, Skylark, Take Five, tangled hair, Tanka Journal, Tanka Splendor, Under the Basho, Women's Monthly.

I thank my friend, poet John Rowe, who kindly read and offered his insights on this collection.

About the Author

Jeanne Lupton, a poet since she learned to read, moved to the San Francisco East Bay from Northern Virginia in 2002 and has been active since then in the poetry community here and in the tanka community worldwide through tanka journals. Her collection, *but then you danced*, which appeared in 2006, and several booklets published since then are included here. This collection represents the first 25 years of her tanka. Jeanne hosted the Second Saturday Poetry and Prose Reading Series at Frank Bette Center for the Arts in Alameda, California, for 13 years. She has given several short solo performances at the Marsh Theater in Berkeley.

Jeanne leads a memoir writing group for seniors on Zoom, is a member of Fresh Ink Poetry Collective and Bay Area Poets Coalition, and writes with Clive Matson's Too Busy to Write group every Tuesday night. She lives at Strawberry Creek Lodge in Berkeley with 150 other elders and her cat BB.

Tanka are two lines longer than haiku and invite the expression of feeling. Traditionally a love poem, tanka is over 1400 years old. Haiku originated when the first three lines of tanka broke off to become their own poetic form. Young people in Japan today text tanka to each other on their cell phones.

I enjoy writing tanka as emotional diary, as a way to peace, as a song of nature, as a reminder of love, as play and work, as connection, as celebration, as gift, as a practice in concision, as a practice in honesty, as a high point in my day, as a way of life. Waiting for the next tanka to come along,

Jeanne Lupton
Berkeley, California
Spring 2021

www.ingramcontent.com/pod-product-compliance
Lightning Source LLC
Chambersburg PA
CBHW022156080426
42734CB00006B/466